THE IMPROVING PROFITABILITY POCKETBOOK

By Anne Hawkins and Clive Turner

Drawings by Phil Hailstone

"Provides a straightforward explanation of 'financial speak', and will be essential reading for all managers."
Michael Millward, HR Training & Development Manager, Newbridge Networks Ltd

"An excellent guide for non-financial managers, as well as a reminder to experienced managers of the key measures for improving performance."
Paul Lester, Group Managing Director, Balfour Beatty Ltd

CONTENTS

INTRODUCTION

ASSESSING PERFORMANCE

How does your business shape up?

Is it financially fit - or flabby?

Could it do better?

HOW DO YOU ASSESS AND IMPROVE BUSINESS FINANCIAL PERFORMANCE?

TOO MANY OPTIONS?

There are plenty of people out there willing to give you advice.

Confused?
Not sure which way to turn?
How do you evaluate
these options and make
the right decisions
for **your** business?

IMPROVING PROFITABILITY

THE METHOD

This Pocketbook can help you improve your business performance by following this programme to financial fitness:

- **The Health Check** - Measuring Financial Performance
- **Fitness Programme** - Improving Financial Performance
- **Keeping in Shape** - Shaping your Business for the Future

HEALTH CHECK

MEASURING FINANCIAL PERFORMANCE

5

MEASURING FINANCIAL PERFORMANCE

WHO AND WHY?

All parties have an interest in financial performance:

- Will I be paid?
- Will I get a dividend?
- Will the shares go up in value?
- Is the business financially secure?
  - Will it survive?
  - Is the product guarantee worth the paper it's written on?

There are appropriate financial measures for each of these. But where do you **start** measuring?

THE ULTIMATE QUESTION

What really tells you how your business is doing?

Start with the ultimate question:

Would you be better off putting your money in the bank?

Start with **PROFITABILITY.**

WHAT IS PROFITABILITY?

Suppose you were offered the opportunity to invest in a venture guaranteeing you a profit of £1,000.

- Would you invest?
- What else would you need to consider?

You would need to know **how much** you have to invest!

Consider the following:

	Profit £	Investment £	Rate of Return
Venture 1	1,000	1,000	100%
Venture 2	1,000	10,000	10%
Venture 3	1,000	100,000	1%

Profitability is the rate of return on your investment!

Note the difference between **profit** and **profitability**.

MEASURING FINANCIAL PERFORMANCE

PROFITABILITY

HOW DO YOU MEASURE IT?

To measure profitability in the business you need to know:

| How much there is invested in the business | Net Capital Employed*
ie: Fixed Assets plus Working Capital* |

and

| How much you have made | Operating Profit*
ie: Profit Before Interest & Tax (PBIT)* |

* For an explanation of these terms see Appendix One.

Profitability is measured as:

$$\frac{\text{Operating Profit}}{\text{Net Capital Employed}} \times 100\%$$

and tells you the rate of return in the business
- how much profit is being made on every £1 invested in the business
- how effective you are at making your investment work!

MEASURING PROFITABILITY

EXAMPLE

'Greasy Joe's' Café

Joe's business makes a profit of £50,000

'Fit Fred's' Gym

Fred's business makes a profit of £25,000

Which business has performed better?
It looks like Greasy Joe's Café. But you can't tell!
Measure their profitability!

MEASURING PROFITABILITY

EXAMPLE

Joe has £250,000 invested in his business.

His profitability is: $\dfrac{£50,000}{£250,000}$ x 100% = 20%

ie: every £1 invested with Joe will earn 20p profit.

Fred has £50,000 invested in his business.

His profitability is: $\dfrac{£25,000}{£50,000}$ x 100% = 50%

ie: every £1 invested with Fred will earn 50p profit.

Joe has a 20% rate of return.
Fred has a 50% rate of return.

So Fred has the 'fitter' business!

PROFITABILITY & EXPANSION

Look how profitability affects your ability to expand.
If Joe wanted to expand and increase his profit to £100,000, he would need to invest another £250,000.

	Joe's Café 1	Joe's Café 2	TOTAL
Profit	£50,000	£50,000	£100,000
Investment	£250,000	£250,000	£500,000

But Fred could **quadruple** his business and his profits to £100,000 by investing just another £150,000.

	Gym 1	Gym 2	Gym 3	Gym 4	TOTAL
Profit	£25,000	£25,000	£25,000	£25,000	£100,000
Investment	£50,000	£50,000	£50,000	£50,000	£200,000

Joe would need to invest another £250,000 bringing his total investment to £500,000.

Fred would need an additional £150,000 bringing his total investment to only £200,000.

Fred could make the same profit as Joe with only 40% of Joe's investment!

MEASURING FINANCIAL PERFORMANCE

ROCE

Profitability is referred to as Return on Capital Employed (or ROCE).

Hence $\text{ROCE} = \dfrac{\text{Operating Profit}}{\text{Net Capital Employed}} \times 100\%$ *(see page 9)*

What does ROCE tell you?

It tells you how much money has been made on every £1 invested in the business.

Is your ROCE good enough?

What else could you have done with the money?
How does your ROCE compare with those alternatives?
Should you sell up and put your money in the bank ...
... or what steps can you take to improve your profitability?

Read on!

RISK V RETURN

When comparing alternative investments it is important to remember to consider the relative risks as well as returns.

The greater the risk, the higher the prospective return must be to justify the risk taken.

Understanding and managing aspects of business risk are dealt with in the section on Keeping in Shape (see pages 47-93).

FITNESS PROGRAMME

THE MULTIPLIER
(How a small change can make a big impact)

THE MULTIPLIER

HOW TO GET FIT

Learn to manage profitability.

$$\text{ROCE} = \frac{\text{Operating Profit}}{\text{Net Capital Employed}} \times 100\% \quad \textit{(see page 13)}$$

You want to improve your ROCE. But where do you start?
Look what goes into the ratio.

Operating Profit: the margins you make on what you sell ...

Net Capital Employed: how much you've had to invest to set up the business
and keep it running ...

How do these relate?
How can you see clearly the actions you need to take?

INTRODUCE SALES INTO THE RATIO AND TURN YOUR BUSINESS INTO A CHAMPION!

INTRODUCING THE MULTIPLIER

In business, profit comes from sales. Introduce sales into the equation and make **The Multiplier** work for you!

$$ROCE = \frac{\text{Operating Profit}}{\text{Net Capital Employed}} \times 100\%$$

Or ROCE *(see Note)* $= \dfrac{\text{SALES}}{\text{Net Capital Employed}} \quad \times \quad \dfrac{\text{Operating Profit}}{\text{SALES}} \times 100\%$

'Asset Turn'   'The Multiplier'   'Return on Sales'

ie: ROCE $=$ Asset Turn $\times$ Return on Sales

How does **that** help?

> ▶ **Note:** Remember your basic algebra!
> When you multiply Asset Turn by Return on Sales the sales will cancel out.

INTRODUCING THE MULTIPLIER

Remember Joe and Fred? *(see page 11)*

Profitability: Joe 20%   Fred 50%.

Fred's business is 'fitter' than Joe's. Why? What does Fred do better than Joe? Introduce the Multiplier and find out!

The information you require:

	Joe's Café	Fred's Gym
Operating Profit	£50,000	£25,000
Net Capital Employed	£250,000	£50,000
and in addition		
Sales	£500,000	£200,000

THE MULTIPLIER

INTRODUCING ROS

In business profit comes from sales

Return on Sales (ROS) = $\dfrac{\text{Operating Profit}}{\text{Sales}}$ x 100% *(see page 17)*

ie: the net margin on sales.

Now calculate this for Joe and Fred. Who makes the better margin on his sales?

	Joe's Café	**Fred's Gym**
$\dfrac{\text{Operating Profit}}{\text{Sales}}$ x 100%	$\dfrac{£50,000}{£500,000}$ x 100%	$\dfrac{£25,000}{£200,000}$ x 100%
Hence ROS =	10%	12½%

Fred produces profit more efficiently from his sales (12½p on every £1 sales) compared with Joe (10p on every £1 sales).

THE MULTIPLIER

INTRODUCING ASSET TURN

Net Capital Employed is required to set up and run the business in order to achieve the sales.

$$\text{Asset Turn} = \frac{\text{Sales}}{\text{Net Capital Employed}} \quad \text{(see page 17)}$$

ie: the number of times the investment was 'turned over' in terms of the sales achieved.

Now calculate this for Joe and Fred. Whose investment works the hardest?

	Joe's Café	Fred's Gym
Sales	£500,000	£200,000
Net Capital Employed	£250,000	£50,000
Hence Asset Turn =	2	4

Fred makes his investment work harder producing £4 of sales for every £1 invested, compared with Joe's £2.

THE MULTIPLIER

WAYS TO IMPROVE

So Fred wins!

	Asset Turn	x	ROS	= ROCE
Joe	2	x	10%	= 20%
Fred	4	x	12½%	= 50%

He is making his investment work harder to produce sales, and is achieving the sales at a higher margin.

So what can Joe do to improve?

- Set himself a profitability (ROCE) target
- Identify ways to improve his Asset Turn
  (see page 25 onwards for a pocketful of ideas)
- Look for ways to increase his ROS
  (see page 37 onwards to get you started)

THE MULTIPLIER

SETTING PROFITABILITY TARGETS

To set your profitability target, select
realistic Asset Turn and Return on
Sales levels. Remember that a
target of, say, 30% ROCE can be
achieved in an infinite number of ways.

ASSET TURN		ROS		ROCE
2	x	15%	=	30%
3	x	10%	=	30%
5	x	6%	=	30%
10	x	3%	=	30%

Which is right for you?

- Does your business require a substantial investment in buildings, machinery, stock,
  etc, to achieve the level of sales? The Asset Turn will then be relatively low.
  Your products must generate a high ROS to 'offset' the low Asset Turn.

- Or does your business achieve high volumes of sales at low margins?
  Then a relatively high Asset Turn must be achieved to 'offset' the low ROS.

*Golden Rule: A business which has a low number for both Asset Turn and ROS will
find it impossible to survive!*

THE MULTIPLIER

MAKE IT WORK FOR YOU

Small changes to both components can have a **dramatic** impact on business profitability **because of the Multiplier**.

Improve your ROCE by tackling both sides of the Multiplier
... and look forward to a multiplied benefit!

Look what it could do for Joe.

	Asset Turn	x	ROS	= ROCE
Existing situation	2	x	10%	= 20%
Joe sells off surplus stock; Asset Turn increases by 10%	2.2	x	10%	= 22% (ROCE up by 10%)
or				
Joe finds a better fish merchant, offering lower prices; ROS improves by 10%	2	x	11%	= 22% (ROCE up by 10%)
Better still, what if Joe achieves both?	2.2	x	11%	= 24.2% (ROCE up by 21%!)

THE MULTIPLIER

MAKE IT WORK FOR YOU

Do you want to improve **your** profitability?

Have you checked your Asset Turn and ROS?

Remember, use the Multiplier to build small changes into dramatic improvements!

Short of ideas of how to boost your Asset Turn and/or ROS?

Read on!

IMPROVING ASSET TURN
(How to make your money work harder)

HOW TO MAKE YOUR MONEY WORK HARDER

Asset Turn $= \dfrac{\text{Sales}}{\text{Net Capital Employed}}$ *(see page 20)*

Interpretation The number of times the investment was 'turned over' in terms of the sales achieved

Objective Maximise the Asset Turn to improve the ROCE

How Either: Reduce your investment whilst maintaining sales
or: Increase sales **without** proportionate increases in your investment

Focus Resource Management

> **Note:** Asset Turn is a general indicator of risk
> - the higher the number the lower the risk
> - the lower the number the higher the funding required to finance growth.
> Don't forget the Asset Turn will increase year on year due to depreciation
> and price increments. Find ways to achieve REAL improvements.

RESOURCE MANAGEMENT

Net Capital Employed is the amount of long-term money invested in the business.
Net Capital Employed is used to provide:

Facilities/Processes   'The Tools to do the Job'   (Fixed Assets)*

Product/Service Investment   'Day to day running costs'   (Working Capital)*

You need to optimise the use of Net Capital Employed within your business.

These terms are explained in more detail in The Balance Sheet Pocketbook.

(27)

CHALLENGING ASSET TURN

To manage the Asset Turn, you must focus on:

- Efficient use of your facilities/processes   (Fixed Assets)
- Effective use of the product/service investment   (Working Capital)
- Sales growth

Look at each of these in turn.

IMPROVING ASSET TURN

MANAGING FACILITY INVESTMENT

Scrutinise the investment you have in your facilities/processes and look to:

- Releasing surplus Fixed Assets
- Reviewing subcontract opportunities *(see Make/Buy page 67)*
- Reviewing multi-shifting facilities, equipment and machines
- Reviewing site rationalisation, consolidation
- Reviewing the approval process and timing of new investments
  (see Investing in Fixed Assets page 47).

WORKING CAPITAL

Working Capital is the net amount invested in the business in the financing of:

- the flow of materials
- the conversion process into your finished product/service
- the credit required to support the sales
  after allowing for external funding through
- the credit given by suppliers.

WORKING CAPITAL CYCLE

Working Capital is usefully portrayed as a cycle of money through the business, starting and finishing with cash.

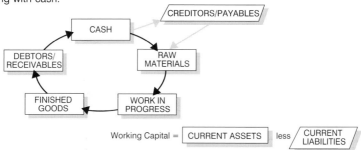

Working Capital = CURRENT ASSETS less CURRENT LIABILITIES

Objective:
Complete the cycle as quickly and as frequently as possible.

Make your Working Capital **WORK!**

IMPROVING ASSET TURN

MANAGING STOCK

Do you need all that stock?

- Review stock-holding policies; lead times; product range
- Look for the balance between volume efficiency and the cost of holding stock
- Consider buying in kits/sub-assemblies rather than building your own
- What about consignment stocks?
  - Can you negotiate with your suppliers for them to hold stock for you on your premises? *(Try to)*
  - Do your customers require you to hold your stock on their premises? *(Try not to)*
- Can you move towards JIT? *(Just-in-Time)*

Note: If you can reduce the unit cost of your product/service then this will:

MANAGING YOUR DEBTORS

The game is not over when you achieve the sale. **Your** money is still invested in the product/service until the customer **pays**. If your customer doesn't pay, you'll regret ever having taken the business on. You must **complete** the Working Capital cycle.

Review your customer credit policies:

- Do you **have** to offer your customer credit? Remember it is a key part of the order negotiation process.
- How do you assess credit-worthiness?
- How do you control the amount of credit in terms of days and amount allowed?
- How do you monitor payment performance?
- How do you deal with overdues?
- Do you have controls in place to stop further deliveries to customers who haven't paid for the last lot?
- Do you ensure that your invoices are accurate?
- Do you avoid part deliveries?

MANAGING YOUR CREDITORS

Remember that it is advantageous to purchase on credit. This reduces the amount of money **you** have to find to run the business, which

 reduces
Net Capital Employed

 increasing
Asset Turn

 improving
ROCE!

However, just not paying your suppliers is short-termist and endangers your future supplies.

Instead look to **manage** creditors:

- Negotiate credit terms as well as price, quality, delivery, etc
- Supplier rationalisation could yield both price and credit term benefits
- Enhance your importance to your suppliers by a 'partnership' approach offering mutual gains

These Working Capital issues are further developed in The Managing Cashflow Pocketbook.

EVERYTHING CONTRIBUTES

Just think!

To achieve a 30% ROCE you need to earn a 30p Operating Profit on **EVERY** £1 invested in the business.

Keep reviewing those facilities, stocks, debtors and creditors.

Is **EVERYTHING**
pulling its weight?

Eliminate surplus investment in Net Capital Employed and improve your profitability.

SALES GROWTH

Don't forget you can also improve your Asset Turn by increasing sales without a proportionate increase in your investment.

Drive your assets harder!

Win more business	Focus on sales with high unit selling prices Manage new product introductions
Get the price right!	Review prices - especially spares, repairs, small orders, additional charges (eg: carriage)
Satisfy the orders!	Eliminate arrears and returns Deliver on time Eliminate machine breakdowns and materials shortages

Objective: Increase sales by improved utilisation of Net Capital Employed.

FITNESS PROGRAMME

IMPROVING RETURN ON SALES
(How to make more whilst spending less)

HOW TO MAXIMISE PROFITABILITY

Return on Sales $= \dfrac{\text{Operating Profit}}{\text{Sales}} \times 100\%$ *(see page 19)*

Interpretation   The Net Margin on sales

Objective   Maximise the ROS to improve the ROCE

Focus   Cost control

Operating Profit = Sales - Cost (Attributable Revenue Expenditure*)

Improving sales has already been dealt with *(see page 36)*.

Cost control and focused cost reduction are invaluable management tools. Substantial improvements can be attained without resorting to major cost cutting programmes. Surprised?

Read on!

* *This is explained in detail in The Balance Sheet Pocketbook.*

IMPROVING RETURN ON SALES

REDUCING COSTS

First of all - the good news! Small decreases in costs have a dramatic effect on ROS!
Why?

Look back to the example on page 23. Joe improves his ROS from 10% to 11% - an
improvement of 10%. By how much do costs have to fall to achieve this?

By 10%? **NO**. **Only 1%!!!**

Why?

	Before	After	
	£'000	£'000	
Sales	500	500	
Cost	450	445	Joe reduces his costs by 1% ...
Operating Profit	50	55	
ROS	10%	11%	... and his ROS goes up by 10%!

*Look at all the tips in the next few pages for ways to find those small cost reductions
which can make such a big difference.*

MANAGING RESOURCES

Manage material costs by:

- Reducing suppliers' prices, by using purchasing power and supplier rationalisation
- Improving materials' usage by eliminating scrap
- Redesigning to eliminate materials consumed in the process
- Recycling surplus or scrap materials

Manage people costs by:

- Reducing absenteeism
- Effective training
- Eliminating non-productive time

A small change can make a big difference!

40

MANAGING OVERHEADS

Examine and reduce your overheads by understanding the cost drivers - the activities.

Managers should focus on:

- Eliminating waste
- Using purchasing power to control prices
- Demanding designs that are cost-effective to make, support and sell
- Challenging the procedures to deliver services, both to internal and external customers, and eliminating activities that do not add value
- Reorganising office layout to facilitate communication
- Implementing management review techniques, eg: Business Process Re-engineering
- Appraising IT for potential activity savings

Control the activity to manage the cost!

IMPROVING SALES GROWTH

Have you followed up the actions for sales growth on page 36?
Here are some more!

- Use quantity discounts but ensure that your customer's projected volumes really exist

- Win more business from your customer; build the partnership through:
  - collaboration
  - sole source
  - preferred supplier status, etc

- Identify and develop competitive advantage:
  - lowest price?
  - product/service differentiation?
  - after sales support?

Understand and exploit market needs.

MANAGING TRADE-OFFS
(Making sure that you gain more on the swings than you lose on the roundabouts)

CONSIDER BOTH COMPONENTS

Understanding the components of ROCE requires that you manage any 'trade-offs'.

Example

To improve Asset Turn, businesses might introduce a settlement discount for prompt payment:

Effect No. 1   Improves Asset Turn   (Reduces debtors)

Effect No. 2   Reduces ROS   (Discount reduces profits)

	Asset Turn		ROS		ROCE
From	4.0	x	10%	=	40%
To	4.2	x	8%	=	33.6%

Is it worth it?

DOUBLE WHAMMIES

Don't forget there is also the opportunity of a double-whammy!
There are actions which can improve both sides of the multiplier at once.

ACTIONS	ASSET TURN	ROS	ROCE
Supplier Rationalisation i. Reduces Prices ii. Increases Credit Period	Improves	Improves	Improves Improves
Increase Capacity through Shift Working: i. Reduces Capital Expenditure and accelerates Depreciation ii. Increases Sales and Overhead Absorption	Improves	Improves	Improves Improves
Increase selling price where you have bargaining power (spares, repairs)	Improves	Improves	Improves (Twice)

45

ROCE MUST BE MANAGED

SUMMARY

- ROCE is a composite ratio and the result of Asset Turn x ROS

- Small improvements to the respective components are compounded by the Multiplier

- The Asset Turn is driven by the way you do business, ie: your process choices (Fixed Assets) and product/service flow (Working Capital)

- The ROS reflects the day to day operation of the business and summarises the impact of pricing and cost control decisions

- Evaluate the trade-offs and exploit the double-whammies: measure the impact on each of the components!

KEEPING IN SHAPE

INVESTING IN FIXED ASSETS
(Capital Expenditure Appraisal)

47

MANAGING CHANGE

So you're now making your investment work harder (Asset Turn) and more efficiently (ROS) - delivering an improved ROCE.

Is that it?

No!

Businesses are dynamic units and are subject to change.

Managers must be able to identify and evaluate the implications of change. Consider the following scenarios:

- Market prices for your products fall
- Your costs increase and you are unable to pass the increase on to your customers
- Machines have to be replaced
- Your business introduces a new product or enters new markets

How do you evaluate such change?

Read on!

TOOLS TO EVALUATE CHANGE

The challenge

How to implement change and continue to improve profitability:

- Identify the key decisions and apply the appropriate techniques

Decisions	**Techniques**
Investing in Facilities/Machines	Capital Expenditure Appraisal
Outsourcing v In-house	Make/Buy
Cost Reduction/Pricing	Profit-Cost-Volume

INVESTING IN FIXED ASSETS

A STRATEGIC DECISION

When the business purchases new facilities/processes (Fixed Assets) this is referred to as 'Capital Expenditure'.

Fixed Assets are bought with the intention of keeping them and using them in the business over a number of years - the 'tools to do the job'. Capital Expenditure is a **strategic decision**; it commits the organisation to the way it is going to carry out its business for many years to come.

What happens if you make the wrong choice, and your competitors get it right? Of course you can change, but it will take time and money to do that. The emphasis must be on challenging the proposed expenditure, asking:

- Have I thought through all the options?
- Have I assessed the implications for my business?
- **Have I got it right?**

INVESTING IN FIXED ASSETS

BUSINESS IMPLICATIONS

NEVER START WITH THE NUMBERS!!
Does the expenditure support/advance the achievement of the agreed business strategy?

Look at the impact on:

Suppliers: ● How will this investment affect your bargaining power with them?

Competitors: ● Will this investment give you a competitive advantage?
● Will it create a barrier to entry for new players?
● Is it a mature or an emerging technology?

And last, but most important of all:

Customers: ● What will it offer your customer?
- more product?   - better quality?
- more variety?   - more reliable delivery?
● Will it enhance your bargaining power?

Remember: **If the customer is not willing to pay for your investment either**
through buying more, or paying more, then you will be left holding
the bill and will need to generate effective cost reduction elsewhere!

51

INVESTING IN FIXED ASSETS

RISK V RETURN

Capital Expenditure commits the investment for the life of the asset. The financial and business risk must be evaluated.

● How quickly do you get your money back?

● How easily could you reverse the decision if circumstances changed?

● Will it require new labour skills?

● Are you introducing new products into a new market (high risk) or into current markets (reduced risk)?

Remember, the larger the investment, the greater the potential risk. Will it be worth it? Does the return warrant the risk?

Underpin your risk assessment with basic sensitivity analysis, ie: 'What if?' scenarios. Assessed the risk? Now proceed to the financial evaluation to measure the return.

 Note: A worked example of a financial evaluation is given in Appendix Two.

INVESTING IN FIXED ASSETS

RELEVANT CASHFLOWS

Most proposals require the business to:

Spend money now   eg: buy a new machine   ⇨ short-term reduction in Asset Turn
for

Future benefits   eg: increased output   ⇨ long-term improvement in
Asset Turn and ROS

The long-term nature of these decisions requires the use of appropriate financial
evaluation techniques.

Firstly, identify the **relevant cashflows** (ie: the cashflows in and out of the business that
would result from the proposal), and the timing of those flows. The financial techniques that
follow rely **entirely** on these cashflows. **The techniques do not refine or improve the
quality of the data. Validate and challenge the input data!**

The output from the evaluation process may suggest an excellent investment - but if
the source data is a 'dream' or inflated to get approval, the performance indicated will
not be delivered.

INVESTING IN FIXED ASSETS

KEEP IT RELEVANT!

You have now built up a profile of the cashflows that will result from the project, and identified the timing of these flows.

A final check on the projected cashflows:

- Do **not** include those that have happened already and have been charged against previous years' profits, eg: R&D
- **Do** include increases to overhead expenses attributable to the proposal
  (Note: replacement machines will be charged with the overheads allocated to the original machine, adjusted for the overall change to total overheads)
- **Do** include all adjustments to Working Capital attributable to the proposals (stocks, debtors and creditors)

Now apply the financial evaluation techniques used by the accountant:

Payback   Net Present Value   Internal Rate of Return

which are explained on the following pages.

Each technique views the proposed investment in a different way. They will often reveal trade-offs for management to consider. In most companies 'hurdle rates' are in place, to reveal high risk proposals.

INVESTING IN FIXED ASSETS

PAYBACK

Payback is the simplest and most common form of financial evaluation.

It is the period of time required for the project cashflows to reimburse the initial outlay.

Expressed as a **time** factor: years/months

Example

A new machine will cost the business £25,000. It will result in cost savings (cash inflows) over the next four years as follows:

	Annual cashflow	Cumulative cashflow
Year 1	£10,000	£10,000
Year 2*	£15,000	£25,000*
Year 3	£18,000	£43,000
Year 4	£20,000	£63,000

Payback period: 2 years*

INVESTING IN FIXED ASSETS

PAYBACK APPRAISED

How does payback help?

- It provides a general indication of risk: the longer the payback period the greater the risk
- It identifies when the project investment will be released for possible re-investment

But

It often distracts management focus from other measures.

Do not base your decision on payback period alone:

- It ignores cashflows beyond the pay-back point - thereby rejecting excellent longer-term projects
- It does not measure the return on the investment

Therefore, use in conjunction with other techniques to allow for 'trade-off' decisions.

TIME & MONEY

Even without inflation, £100 now is worth more to you than £100 in the future.

Why?

Because you could invest the £100 and earn interest on it!

If interest rates are at 10%:

    After 1 year the £100 will become   £110
    After 2 years the £100 will become   £121
    After 3 years the £100 will become   £133, etc

So if you spend £100 on a machine now and make savings (cash inflows) of £100 over the next 3 years ... is this good enough?

Surely you need to generate at least £133 cash, or you would have been better off leaving your money in the bank!

What if you have to borrow the £100 at 10%?

You will need £133 cash to repay the loan!

INVESTING IN FIXED ASSETS

NET PRESENT VALUE

To take timing differences and the cost of money into account, projected cashflows are discounted to identify the Net Present Value.

If the projected cashflow is an inflow of £4,000 after two years, what would be the Net Present Value of the £4,000? That is, how much would you need to invest today at 10% interest to provide £4,000 in two years' time.

$$£4,000 \quad \times \quad \frac{1}{1.1} \quad \times \quad \frac{1}{1.1} \quad = \quad £3,306$$

So, receiving £4,000 in two years' time is equivalent to receiving £3,306 today.

INVESTING IN FIXED ASSETS

NET PRESENT VALUE

EXAMPLE

You plan to buy a machine costing £10,000 which will enable you to sell extra products at reduced costs, resulting in additional cash inflows of:

> Year 1   £3,000
> Year 2   £4,000
> Year 3   £5,000

The proposal is to be discounted at 10%.

> **Note:** Each business will determine its own discount rate (or 'cost of capital').
> It must consider the cost of the alternative sources of finance open to it, the risk profile
> of the markets and future growth requirements.

INVESTING IN FIXED ASSETS

NET PRESENT VALUE

DISCOUNT RATES

Step 1: Establish the discount factors

Discount factors at 10% will be :

Year 1 $\dfrac{1}{1.1}$ $= 0.909$

Year 2 $\dfrac{1}{1.1}$ x $\dfrac{1}{1.1}$ $= 0.826$

Year 3 $\dfrac{1}{1.1}$ x $\dfrac{1}{1.1}$ x $\dfrac{1}{1.1}$ $= 0.751$

> **Note:** These factors can be obtained directly from discount tables.
> Most PC based software provides the discount factor as required.

NET PRESENT VALUE

APPLICATION

Step 2: Apply the discount factors to each year's cashflow

Year	Cashflow	Discount Factor	NPV
	a	b	c = (axb)
1	£3,000	0.909	£2,727
2	£4,000	0.826	£3,304
3	£5,000	0.751	£3,755
		Total	£9,786

ie: Receiving £3,000 in 1 year's time
plus £4,000 in 2 years' time
and £5,000 in 3 years' time
has a Net Present Value of £9,786.

INVESTING IN FIXED ASSETS

NET PRESENT VALUE

INTERPRETATION

Step 3: Compare the NPV of the total cashflow to the project investment required.

		£
i.	NPV of the cashflow	9,786
less		
ii.	Initial project investment	10,000
		(214)

The company will be £214 worse off if it invests in the project rather than accepting the equivalent cashflow from a secure investment in the bank.

Interpretation: Proposals with positive NPVs are acceptable **on this criterion**
Proposals with negative NPVs will be rejected

Be careful: Just like Payback, NPV has its limitations:
- it takes no account of the scale of the project
- it can be difficult to use when projects have different timescales

Don't forget to use the different techniques and look for the trade-offs.

INTERNAL RATE OF RETURN

The rate of return that the project is expected to yield is called the Internal Rate of Return (IRR).
Using the example on page 59 discounted at 8.9%:

Year	Cashflow £	Discount Factor 8.9%	NPV £
1	3,000	.918	2,754
2	4,000	.844	3,376
3	5,000	.774	3,870
		NPV of the cashflow	10,000
		Equals project investment	£10,000 **Hence, IRR = 8.9%**

So the IRR is the discount factor which discounts the cashflow to equal the project
investment. (In practice the IRR is calculated by computer software - for an example of
manual calculation see Appendix Two.)

INVESTING IN FIXED ASSETS

INTERNAL RATE OF RETURN

INTERPRETATION

The IRR tells you:

- The break-even cost of capital for the project; if your discount rate (see page 59) is above the IRR the proposal would be rejected: if it is below, the project would be accepted

- The compound interest rate the bank needs to offer you to compete with the project, if the alternative is to leave the money in the bank

Be careful: Just like Payback and NPV, IRR has its limitations

Don't forget to use the different techniques and look for the trade-offs. Talk to your accountant.

INVESTING IN FIXED ASSETS

SUMMARY

Capital Expenditure is about long-term commitment. Ask yourself:

- Does the proposal make strategic sense?
- What will it do to my business - and the people I do business with?
- Have I brainstormed all the possible options?
- Have I assessed the risks - against which I can judge the returns?
- Is the data used in my financial evaluation
  - relevant? - realistic?
- Does the proposal meet the required hurdles for:
  - Payback? - NPV? - IRR?
- If there are competing projects - have I examined the trade-offs?

The Golden Rule: *Ask yourself, if it meant committing your **own** money, would you go ahead?*

KEEPING IN SHAPE

MAKE/BUY DECISIONS

(Do we do this ourselves - or pay someone
else to do it for us?)

MAKE/BUY DECISIONS

THINK LONG-TERM

Make or buy decisions are NOT simple cost comparisons!

Out-sourcing might reduce costs in the short term; but what are the long-term implications for the business?

Conversely, it may be beneficial to outsource even at a cost in excess of your apparent in-house cost!

Make or buy decisions must examine the impact on the business and the impact on the **total** financial performance.

- **Business Issues:** Be careful what you might give away; it is essential to ensure that your supplier does not become a competitor

- **Financial Issues:** Cost comparisons measure the impact on ROS only; it is essential to measure also the implications for Fixed Assets, stocks and creditors, ie: the impact on Asset Turn
  (Remember ROCE = Asset Turn x ROS)

Make or buy decisions can significantly change profitability!

MAKE/BUY DECISIONS

CONSIDER BUSINESS IMPLICATIONS

Don't start with the numbers!   Start with the business implications.

How will the proposal affect your business?

- Is it in line with your business longer-term plans? *(Strategic fit)*
- Will you be handing over a critical aspect of your business to a supplier?
  (Competitive advantage)
- What impact will it have on the nature and scale of your business?
  (Operations investment)
- How will it affect your organisation as a whole? *(Support systems)*

Each of these is now explained.

MAKE/BUY DECISIONS

STRATEGIC FIT

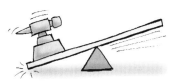

Check that the make/buy decision is consistent with your business plan. Consider the effect/impact it will have on:

- Your relationship with suppliers
- The risk of developing a competitor
- The likelihood of new entrants to your market segment
- The rate and impact of a change in technology
- The risk of product substitution
- The relationship with customers
- Your competitive position

How will it affect the relationships between the business and its competitive environment?

> **Note:** Remember your basic physics! For every action there is an equal and opposite reaction. Consider: how will the competition react?

COMPETITIVE ADVANTAGE

- The make/buy decision must not result in subcontracting the critical success factor essential to winning orders!

- Order winning criteria must be retained in-house, and the business must seek to attain world-best performance of the relevant critical success factor(s)

- Competitive advantage dependent on a supplier is not sustainable, and potentially will grow a winning competitor

- Items which **are** subcontracted must be managed!

OPERATIONS INVESTMENT

Moving work in or out of the business will have implications for the type and scale of capabilities required.

Capacity - will moving the work result in under-utilisation of capacity, or the need for additional capacity?

Specialisation - how will the make/buy decision impact on the type of facility required - more specialised high risk technology; more highly skilled labour?

Technology - is the technology mature or is it high risk emerging technology?

Life-cycle - at what stage of the product life cycle is the relevant product/service
- star? - cow?
- dog? - wild card?

It is essential to understand clearly the impact of the make/buy decision on the operational strategy of the business.

SUPPORT SYSTEMS

The make/buy decision impacts on the support structure required within the business, eg: subcontracting component manufacture will have an impact on:

- purchasing
- planning
- stores
- maintenance programmes

Keeping everything in-house results in a complex support structure and control systems

- ➪ high fixed cost
- ➪ high risk, profit-sensitive to changes in sales volume (see page 81 onwards)
- ➪ longer lead-times
- ➪ inflexible systems

Subcontracting reverses the profile

- ➪ converts fixed costs into variable costs
- ➪ shares the risk (with suppliers)
- ➪ reduces lead-times

Focus your business on your order winning criteria! What must you do best?

MAKE/BUY DECISIONS

FINANCIAL IMPLICATIONS

So you now understand the business implications of your proposal and are ready to do the financial comparison.

Is it simply in-house cost v supplier's quote?

No!

- Will all the in-house cost be saved if you subcontract?

- What about the business investment? How will the decision impact on the Net Capital Employed (Fixed Assets and Working Capital) required?

- What about cash? Will the decision generate or consume cash?

- What about financial risk? Will your resultant business be more or less risky?

- **What about profitability?**

MAKE/BUY DECISIONS

COST COMPARISON

If work is subcontracted the financial structure of the business will change.

The current raw materials, labour and overhead costs will become bought-in costs (which will also include your supplier's profit!).

Be careful when comparing the costs.

Not all of the overheads included in the in-house cost will be saved by subcontracting. Consider, for example, fixed costs which have been apportioned to the product, eg: rent, depreciation, stores, etc. If you subcontract, will these costs change?

The golden rule is to identify clearly the impact of the decision on the cost-base:

- Which costs can be released?
- Which costs will continue?
- Which costs will increase (eg: purchasing)?

MAKE/BUY DECISIONS

BUSINESS INVESTMENT

The make/buy decision will affect the amount and
type of investment required.

Facilities - review buildings, plant,
vehicles, etc
- what could be released?

Working Capital - quantify the impact on stock
and creditors
- note the benefits of subcontracting
where you release stock and secure
increased creditors!

Reducing the business investment
- will release cash (see page 77)
- will improve profit performance by reducing financing costs (eg: interest)
- will improve Asset Turn
- will improve profitability

MAKE/BUY DECISIONS

CASH

The decision to subcontract will improve the cash position of the business by:

- Increasing profits (where there is a cost saving)
- Releasing surplus Fixed Assets
- Reducing stock
- Increasing creditors

In-house manufacture requires funding!
Subcontracting is a cash generator; the Asset Turn increases.

MAKE/BUY DECISIONS

RISK PROFILE

Make/buy decisions affect the financial risk profile of the business.

Subcontracting   - converts fixed costs into variable costs

- reduces the business investment required, giving the opportunity to eliminate excessive borrowing/loans

- results in improved profits through reduced financial burdens (eg: interest)

- allows the business to focus on the order winners; what it must be best at

   Reduces financial risk!

MAKE/BUY DECISIONS

PROFITABILITY

Just look what subcontracting can do to your ROCE.

Current position	*ASSET TURN*		*ROS*		*ROCE*
	2	x	5%	=	10%

Make/buy decision:

A cost comparison between in-house and subcontract component manufacture
showed no apparent cost saving from moving the work outside.
However, the decision was taken based on the other financial benefits.

Continued

MAKE/BUY DECISIONS

PROFITABILITY

Current position	*ASSET TURN*		*ROS*		*ROCE*
	2	x	5%	=	10%

Impact of outsourcing

FIXED ASSETS   ⬇ Decreased

STOCK   ⬇ Decreased

CREDITORS   ⬆ Increased

Hence   ⬇ Net Capital Employed fell by 50%, and

   ⬆ Asset Turn doubled (2 to 4)

Outcome:	4	x	5%	=	20%

Make/buy is much more than simple cost comparison!

KEEPING IN SHAPE

PROFIT-COST-VOLUME
(Improving business agility)

PROFIT-COST-VOLUME

BUSINESS AGILITY

Managing profitability on a day to day basis is extremely difficult. The business is a dynamic model:

- Sales change
- Costs change
- New competitors join the race, etc

Managers are still expected to deliver the required profitability.

Do you really understand **your** business? What would be the impact on profitability of:

- A price war with your competitors?
- Doubling your market share?
- An increase in your rent?
- Re-sourcing to a cheaper supplier?

How do you manage profitability on a day to day basis?

Read on!

PROFIT-COST-VOLUME

MANAGING CHANGE

Remember, you must balance risk v return (see page 14).

Businesses operate in a world of rapid change.

To manage business profitability you need to understand your cost and revenue structure.

Profit-Cost-Volume (P-C-V) is a useful technique for evaluating both the existing business position, the impact of change on costs and/or revenue, and the resultant ROS. Looking at the impact on profitability?

Be careful! Don't forget to look also at the implications of your proposals on the Asset Turn.

PROFIT-COST-VOLUME

WORKED EXAMPLE

Sarah runs her own business 'Magic Carpets'.

Her budget for next year is:

	£'000	
Sales	1,000	(2,000 carpets @ £500 each)
Costs	900	
Profit	100	

Her managers have put a number of suggestions to her:

Marketing: Advertise to increase sales!
Quality: Improve quality and increase your market share!

How can she understand and demonstrate the impact of these proposals?
Use the P-C-V approach!

PROFIT-COST-VOLUME

CLASSIFY COSTS

To understand the current business:

Step 1 Identify your Fixed and Variable costs.

Fixed Costs include all revenue expenditure which is incurred on a time basis and does not depend on the level of sales, eg: rent, salaries, depreciation, buildings, insurance.

Variable Costs are those costs which increase or decrease with fluctuations in sales, eg: direct materials, direct labour, sales commission, packaging.

Sarah classifies her costs as:

	£'000
Fixed	400
Variable	500
Total	900

PROFIT-COST-VOLUME

PROFIT GRAPH

Step 2 Construct a **Profit Graph**.

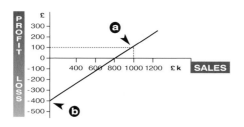

Plot 'a' which is the existing (or budgeted) level of profit at the appropriate level of sales.

Plot 'b' on the vertical axis at the value of fixed costs.

Note: This is the maximum loss the business could make by incurring the fixed costs but making no sales.

Join a) and b).

The Profit Graph provides a useful picture depicting the P-C-V relationships of the business.

Make it work for you!

PROFIT-COST-VOLUME

BREAK-EVEN POINT & MARGIN OF SAFETY

Step 3 Identify the **Break-Even Point** and the **Margin of Safety.**

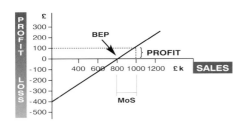

Break-Even Point (BEP)

- The level of sales at which sales income equals revenue costs

- The business makes neither a profit nor a loss

Margin of Safety (MoS)

- The proportion of sales achieved in excess of the break-even point

Therefore, Sarah needs to sell £800,000 to break even, and she has a Margin of Safety of 20%

The higher the MoS
- **the lower the risk**
- **the higher the profit**

The lower the MoS
- **the higher the risk**
- **the lower the profit**

PROFIT-COST-VOLUME

MANAGING CHANGE

What would Sarah like to be able to do?

Increase her profit and increase her margin of safety.

How can she achieve this?

In many different ways!

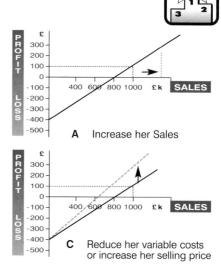

A Increase her Sales

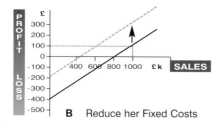

B Reduce her Fixed Costs

C Reduce her variable costs or increase her selling price

PROFIT-COST-VOLUME

EVALUATING CHOICES

Remember her managers' suggestions? Would they help?

Marketing: 'Spend £50k on an advertising campaign which will increase sales by 25%.'

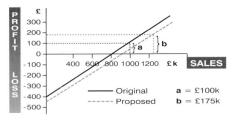

— Original   **a** = £100k
-- - Proposed   **b** = £175k

Proposal:		£'000
Sales:	£1,000k +25% =	1250
V.C.:	£500k +25% =	625
F.C.:	£400k +£50k =	450
Profit		175

Financial Profile:
Profit would increase to £175k.
The BEP would become
£900k of sales.
The MoS would increase to 28%.
ROS would increase from 10% to 14%.

Conclusion:
If the sales increase is real and Asset Turn is held, profitability will increase by 40%

PROFIT-COST-VOLUME

EVALUATING CHOICES

Quality: 'Improve market share by offering a better quality carpet. Spend an extra £25 on each carpet (ie: increase variable costs by 10%) and see the sales volume increase by 20% whilst holding fixed costs at £400k!'

The revised profit graph would be:

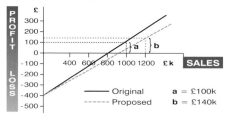

— Original   **a** = £100k
---- Proposed   **b** = £140k

Proposal:		£'000
Sales	£1,000k + 20%	1200
V.C.:	(£500k + 10%) + 20%	660
F.C.		400
Profit		140

Financial Profile:
Profit would increase to £140k.
The BEP would become £889k of sales.
The MoS would increase to 26%.
ROS would increase from 10% to 11.7%.

Conclusion: If the sales increase is real and Asset Turn is held, this will result in increased profitability.

PROFIT-COST-VOLUME

EVALUATING CHOICES

After further investigations Sarah believes she could combine the proposals by improving quality (variable costs up by 10%) and increasing advertising (fixed costs up by £50k), with the result that sales would increase by £500k (50% volume increase).

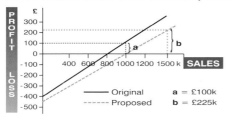

Conclusion: If the sales increase is real and Asset Turn can be held, there will be a 50% improvement in profitability.

Proposal		£'000
Sales	£1000k + £500k =	1,500
VC	£500k + 10% + 50% =	825
FC	£400k + £50k =	450
Profit		225

Financial Profile
Profit would increase to £225k
The BEP would become £1000k of sales
The MoS would increase to 33%
ROS would increase from 10% to 15%
(ie: an increase of 50%)

91

SUMMARY

Profit-Cost-Volume is a useful tool for evaluating and illustrating the financial impact of business proposals.

The technique can also be applied in a non-graphic method using a series of financial controls as explained in Appendix Three.

The profit graph is an excellent tool to communicate to staff the current financial profile, and the operating implications.

But don't forget to watch that Asset Turn as well!

KEEPING IN SHAPE

CONCLUSION

Feeling fitter?
Is your business now in better shape?
Don't slip back into bad habits!

Keep up those routines!

Step 1	The Health Check	-	What is your ROCE now?
Step 2	The Fitness Programme	-	Stretch the limits!
		-	Use the Multiplier to deliver even better results
Step 3	Keeping in Shape	-	Use change to your advantage and take your business into the Premier Division

APPENDICES

APPENDIX ONE

BUSINESS FINANCIAL MODEL
SOURCE OF FUNDS

- Businesses need long-term finance

- This comes from
  - Shareholders
  - Lenders
  - Reinvestment of profits

Accountant's term:
- Share capital
- Loan capital
- Retained profits

SHARE CAPITAL	LOAN CAPITAL	RETAINED PROFITS
SOURCE OF FUNDS		

The Source of Funds is referred to as **Net Capital Employed**

BUSINESS FINANCIAL MODEL

USE OF FUNDS

- The long-term finance is used to provide

  Accountant's term
  - Facilities/processes   - Fixed assets
  - Products/services   - Working capital

SHARE CAPITAL	LOAN CAPITAL	RETAINED PROFITS

SOURCE OF FUNDS

USE OF FUNDS

FACILITIES / PROCESSES	PRODUCTS / SERVICES
FIXED ASSETS	WORKING CAPITAL

The Use of Funds is referred to as **Net Assets Employed**

APPENDIX ONE

BUSINESS FINANCIAL MODEL

MAKING PROFIT

- By using the fixed assets, the working capital investment generates products that can be sold

- Once **all** costs have been met and interest, tax and dividend allowed for, then any profit left over can be reinvested into the business

SHARE CAPITAL	LOAN CAPITAL	RETAINED PROFITS

SOURCE OF FUNDS

USE OF FUNDS

FACILITIES / PROCESSES	PRODUCTS / SERVICES
FIXED ASSETS	WORKING CAPITAL

Depreciation

Sales

Less: Attributable Cost

Operating Profit *

Less: Interest

Less: Tax

Earnings

Dividend	Retained Profits

* Operating Profit (often referred to as PBIT - Profit before Interest and Tax) is the level of profit resulting from this year's sales after deducting all expenses, but before interest, tax and dividends.

This model is developed step by step in The Balance Sheet Pocketbook

98

APPENDIX TWO

CAPITAL EXPENDITURE APPRAISAL

WORKED EXAMPLE

G. Rowth is evaluating purchasing a new machine which will cost £95,000 with an additional £5,000 for installation. This will enable him to produce a new product for which he has had a market research study done, costing £2,000. The projected life-cycle of the product is 3 years.

	Projected Sales	Incremental Product Costs (excluding Depreciation)
	£'000	£'000
Year 1	100	50
Year 2	120	60
Year 3	60	40

Training and promotion costs in the first year will be £10,000. In addition, £10,000 p.a. of existing running costs will be allocated to the product. At the end of the 3 years the machine could be sold for £5,000.

> **Note:** In practice you also need to take into account changes in Working Capital. The discount rate for his business is 10%.

APPENDIX TWO

CAPITAL EXPENDITURE APPRAISAL

WORKED EXAMPLE

Relevant Cashflows

	Now £'000	Year 1 £'000	Year 2 £'000	Year 3 £'000	
Purchase of new machine	− 95				
Installation Costs	− 5				
Market Research					Not included *a
Sales		+ 100	+ 120	+ 60	
Incremental Costs		− 50	− 60	− 40	
Training and Promotion		− 10			
Existing Running Costs					Not included *b
Sale of Machine				+ 5	
	− 100	+ 40	+ 60	+ 25	

*a   This has already been spent - and charged against profit in previous years.
*b   This is merely an apportionment of costs that will be incurred whether they proceed
    with the project or not.

CAPITAL EXPENDITURE APPRAISAL

WORKED EXAMPLE

1. Payback

	Cash Inflows £'000	Cumulative Inflows £'000
Initial Outlay £100,000		
Year 1	40	40
Year 2	60	100*
Year 3	25	125

* Payback = 2 years

2. Net Present Value

	Net Cashflow a	Discount Factor @ 10% b	NPV c (=axb)
Year 1	£40,000	0.909	£ 36,360
Year 2	£60,000	0.826	£ 49,560
Year 3	£25,000	0.751	£ 18,775
			£ 104,695

Less: Initial Outlay £ 100,000

NPV of the Project + £ 4,695

As the NPV is positive, on this criterion the project is acceptable.

CAPITAL EXPENDITURE APPRAISAL

WORKED EXAMPLE

3. Internal Rate of Return

The IRR is the discount rate at which the project 'breaks even'. At 10% the project is acceptable. Try, say, 12%.

	Net Cashflow a	Discount Factor @ 12% b	NPV c (=axb)
Year 1	£40,000	0.893	£ 35,720
Year 2	£60,000	0.797	£ 47,820
Year 3	£25,000	0.712	£ 17,800
			£ 101,340
		Less: Initial Outlay	£ 100,000
		NPV of the project +	£ 1,340

At 12% the project is still acceptable.

At 13% the NPV of the project becomes: – £297.
(Try it and see!)
Hence by interpolation the IRR would be: $12\% + \dfrac{1,340}{1,340 + 297} = 12.8\%$

ie: The cost of capital could rise to 12.8% before you would change your mind about accepting this project.

CAPITAL EXPENDITURE APPRAISAL

WORKED EXAMPLE - INTERPRETATION

1. Payback

You would 'get back' your money in 2 years, releasing it to be invested elsewhere.

2. Net Present Value

At a 10% discount rate, the business will be £4,695 better off, in today's money terms, if it proceeds with the project.

3. Internal Rate of Return

If you were to choose between going ahead with this project or leaving the money in the bank, the bank would have to offer you at least 12.8% compound interest to 'beat' the project.

Do not forget, however, that risk and return must be carefully weighed.

And don't forget those business issues:
- Does the proposal fit the business plan?
- Have all the options been considered?

Check these assumptions again - are they realistic?

PROFIT–COST–VOLUME

FINANCIAL CONTROLS

The financial profile can be determined by measuring the following:

PV ratio $\qquad = \dfrac{\text{Sales - Variable Cost}}{\text{Sales}} \times 100\%$

The PV ratio is an important control which indicates the rate of profit growth once the business has broken even, ie: it determines the gradient of the line on the profit graph.

Break-Even Point $\qquad = \dfrac{\text{Fixed Costs}}{\text{PV ratio}}$

Margin of Safety $\qquad = \dfrac{\text{Sales - Break-Even Point}}{\text{Sales}} \times 100\%$

Operating Profit $\qquad = $ PV ratio $\times$ Margin of Safety $\times$ Sales value

PROFIT–COST–VOLUME

FINANCIAL CONTROLS

Using the proposals made on pages 89-91:

	ORIGINAL POSITION	MARKETING PROPOSAL	QUALITY PROPOSAL	COMBINED PROPOSAL
PV ratio:	$\dfrac{£1000k-£500k}{£1000k}$	$\dfrac{£1250k-£625k}{£1250k}$	$\dfrac{£1200k-£660k}{£1200k}$	$\dfrac{£1500k-£825k}{£1500k}$
	= 50%	= 50%	= 45%	= 45%
B.E.P.:	$\dfrac{£400k}{50\%}$	$\dfrac{£450k}{50\%}$	$\dfrac{£400k}{45\%}$	$\dfrac{£450k}{45\%}$
	= £800k Sales	= £900k	= £889k	= £1000k
M.o.S.:	$\dfrac{£1000k-£800k}{£1000k}$	$\dfrac{£1250k-£900k}{£1250k}$	$\dfrac{£1200k-£889k}{£1200k}$	$\dfrac{£1500k-£1000k}{£1500k}$
	= 20%	= 28%	= 26%	= 33%
Operating Profit:	50% x £200k = £100k	50% x £350k = £175k	45% x £311k = £140k	45% x £500k = £225k

GLOSSARY OF TERMS

Asset Turn	The number of times the investment, i.e. **Net Capital Employed** is 'turned over' in respect to sales.
Break-Even Point (BEP)	The level of sales at which the sales income equals revenue costs.
Contribution Rate	See **Profit to Volume Ratio**.
Debtors Days	The number of days credit taken by customers, i.e. $\dfrac{\text{Debtors}}{\text{Average Daily Credit Sales}}$
Discounted Cashflow (DCF)	The calculation of the net present value of a projected cashflow by the application of a discount factor.
Fixed Assets	Facilities or Processes - tools to do the job.
Fixed Costs	Items of revenue expenditure which are incurred independent of volume and are charged on a time basis, eg: Rent, Lease Charges, Depreciation.
Internal Rate of Return (IRR)	The rate of return which would be yielded by a project.
Margin of Safety (MoS)	The amount by which sales exceed the **Break-Even Point** usually expressed as a percentage of the total sales.
Net Capital Employed	The Accountant's expression for the long-term investment in the business.

APPENDIX FOUR

GLOSSARY OF TERMS

Operations Gearing	The **Break-Even Point** as a percentage of total sales.
Operating Profit	Sales less attributable costs (also known as Profit Before Interest and Tax: (PBIT).
Payback Period	The period of time required for the accumulation of project cashflow to equal the project investment.
Profitability	The rate of return on the capital employed (see **Return on Capital Employed**).
Profit to Volume Ratio (PV Ratio)	The contribution (selling price less **Variable Cost**) expressed as a percentage of the selling price. Often referred to as the **Contribution Rate.**
Return on Capital Employed (ROCE)	The **Operating Profit** expressed as a percentage of the **Net Capital Employed.** Often referred to as Return on Investment (ROI) or Return on Net Assets (RONA).
Return On Sales	The **Operating Profit** as a percentage of sales. Often referred to as Net Margin.
Stock Turn	The number of times stock is turned over into sales. i.e. $\dfrac{\text{Sales}}{\text{Stock}}$ More usually expressed as a 'number of days' stockholding and often related to Cost of Goods Sold**.**
Variable Costs	Items of revenue expenditure which increase incrementally with each further unit of product/service sold, eg: Direct Materials, Direct Labour, Direct Expenses.
Working Capital	Funds used to provide the flow of materials, services and credit. (Current Assets less Current Liabilities).

PYRAMID OF RATIOS

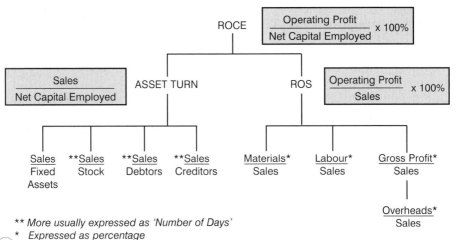

ROCE — $\dfrac{\text{Operating Profit}}{\text{Net Capital Employed}} \times 100\%$

$\dfrac{\text{Sales}}{\text{Net Capital Employed}}$ ASSET TURN

ROS — $\dfrac{\text{Operating Profit}}{\text{Sales}} \times 100\%$

$\dfrac{\text{Sales}}{\text{Fixed Assets}}$ **$\dfrac{\text{Sales}}{\text{Stock}}$ **$\dfrac{\text{Sales}}{\text{Debtors}}$ **$\dfrac{\text{Sales}}{\text{Creditors}}$

$\dfrac{\text{Materials*}}{\text{Sales}}$ $\dfrac{\text{Labour*}}{\text{Sales}}$ $\dfrac{\text{Gross Profit*}}{\text{Sales}}$

$\dfrac{\text{Overheads*}}{\text{Sales}}$

** More usually expressed as 'Number of Days'

* Expressed as percentage

About the Authors

Anne Hawkins, BA, ACMA is a Management Accountant with a first class honours degree in Business Studies. Anne has progressed from this strong knowledge base to gain senior management accounting experience within consumer and industrial product industries. As a Training Consultant she develops and presents finance programmes to Directors and Managers from all sections of industry.

Clive Turner, ACMA, MBCS is Managing Director of Structured Learning Programmes Ltd, established in 1981 to provide management consultancy and training services. Clive works with management to develop strategic business options. He participates in the evaluation process: designs the appropriate organisation structure and provides management development to support the implementation process. Clive continues to have extensive experience in delivering financial modules within Masters Programmes in the UK and overseas. For details of support materials available to help trainers and managers run finance courses in-company, contact the authors at Tall Trees, Barkers Lane, Wythall, Birmingham, West Midlands B47 6BS

© Anne Hawkins and Clive Turner 1997.
This edition published in 1997 by Management Pocketbooks Ltd.
Laurel House, Station Approach, Alresford, Hants SO24 9JH, U.K.
Printed in U.K. Reprinted 1999, 2002.

ISBN 1 870471 44 X

ORDER FORM

Your details

Name _____

Position _____

Company _____

Address _____

_____

Telephone _____

Fax _____

E-mail _____

VAT No. (EC companies) _____

Your Order Ref _____

Please send me:

		No. copies
The Improving Profitability Pocketbook		
The _____ Pocketbook		
The _____ Pocketbook		
The _____ Pocketbook		
The _____ Pocketbook		

Order by Post

MANAGEMENT POCKETBOOKS LTD
LAUREL HOUSE, STATION APPROACH, ALRESFORD,
HAMPSHIRE SO24 9JH UK

Order by Phone, Fax or Internet

Telephone: +44 (0)1962 735573
Facsimile: +44 (0)1962 733637
E-mail: sales@pocketbook.co.uk
Web: www.pocketbook.co.uk

Customers in USA should contact:
Stylus Publishing, LLC, 22883 Quicksilver Drive,
Sterling, VA 20166-2012
Telephone: 703 661 1581 or 800 232 0223
Facsimile: 703 661 1501 E-mail: styluspub@aol.com